Lypptuss the Gum Tree Dragon

You Too Can Have Friends

Grace Kennedy
Dwayne Kennedy

Dr Dee Books

Publication

Lypptuss the Gum Tree Dragon: You Too Can Have Friends © 2020 Grace Kennedy, Dwayne Kennedy, Joseph Bowers. All Rights Reserved. No part of this publication may be reproduced or transmitted in any form or by any means, electronic or mechanical, including photocopying, recording, or by any information retrieval and storage system, without prior written permission of the publisher.

Published by Dr Dee Books
An Imprint of Ability Therapy Specialists Pty Ltd
PO Box 4065, Armidale, New South Wales, Australia 2350
ISBN: 978-1-925034-17-2 [Hardcover]

Keywords: Children, Youth, Adult, Story, Tale, Dragon, Myth, Legend, Artwork, Indigenous, Aboriginal, First Nation, Australian, Canadian, Birthday, Friendship, Friend, Loneliness, Solitude, Social Isolation, Sadness, Depression, Stress, Anxiety, Healing

Disclaimer: This book is produced for entertainment purposes only and is not an authoritative source of information. The author's views do not, nor can they be construed to, represent any other person, community, or entity, including the publisher. Readers ought to seek direct medical advice as your authoritative source of information. The publisher disclaims all liability for all claims, expenses, losses, damages and costs any person may incur as a result of the information contained in this publication, for any reason, being inaccurate, or incomplete in any way, or incapable of or achieving any purpose. These statements do not disclaim statutory obligations as deemed necessary under the law.

Reading Level: This book is produced for primary school levels one to six.

About this Book

Lypptuss the Gum Tree Dragon: You Too Can Have Friends, is a heartwarming story for hearts young and not so young. A beautiful family treasure, this book is based on a long-protected and thirty-year-old manuscript. The drawings had showed a lovely yellow patina as a loving sign of age, timelessness, and beauty. Digitally reproduced and enhanced, the original artwork is by Dwayne and complements the story written by Grace many years ago. It was her dream to see this work shared with others. Joseph provided editing, layout, design, and contributions to the text.

About the Authors

Grace Kennedy is a mother, grandmother, and great grandmother. Dwayne Kennedy is a Counsellor and an Early Childhood Specialist. Joseph Bowers is a Psychotherapist and Behaviour Specialist.

Dedication

Jo-Anna Mary

About Lypptuss

Named after the Eucalyptus Gum Tree, 'Lypptuss' is one very special and mystical dragon who comes to children young and not so young in the Dreamtime of Life. A Healing Dragon, Lypptuss can be found where emotions are at the surface, and people are trying to be their best. She is, at heart, very kind and beautiful. This is her very first ever book. She is so amazingly excited to share this special day with you… Her first ever Birthday.

ONCE UPON A TIME
There was a DRAGON named LYPPTUSS.

This was a very special day.
It was Lypptuss' BIRTHDAY!

But Lypptuss had NOT ONE FRIEND in all the world.
She was feeling very lonely.

She said to herself,
"Today, I am going to find myself a FRIEND!"

Lypptuss was a GOOD DRAGON.
But she was a very UGLY dragon too!

Or so, she had been told…

On this SPECIAL DAY
Lypptuss decided to wander in the bush…

The first creatures she came to
Were TWO TADPOLES and a FROG.

She asked, "Will you PLEASE be my friends?"

The two tadpoles, and the frog remained SILENT…

They just looked at Lypptuss
Like she had the most UGLY head!

Lypptuss said, "Today is my birthday!"

The tadpoles and the frog said with one loud voice,
"No way! You are just too BIG and too UGLY!"

Lypptuss walked away very SAD…

Then a GOOD THOUGHT came into her mind…
"I wonder what FRIEND we can find?"
Lypptuss then trotted off again, feeling much better

She came to a MIGHTY GUM TREE.
With branches stretching as far as you can see!
Guess who she saw?! Can you find him?

Yes!!! A Wise Koala Bear in an Old Gum Tree!
Lypptuss was very hope filled in her heart.

She asked, "Dear Wise Koala, will you be my FRIEND?
For today is my BIRTHDAY!"

"No way!" Said Koala. "You are just too UGLY! Go away!"
Now Lypptuss felt very, very SAD… So, she trotted away…

Next, poor sad Lypptuss met a very BIG bird…
A rather huge BIRD, you ever did see.
Oh me, Oh my, how absurd can this be?

Feeling uncertain, afraid, and lonely,
And most certainly not FREE…
Lypptuss the Lonely Dragon stuttered these words,
"Please be my FRIEND, Dear Pelican Sir Bird.
Today is my BIRTHDAY, and not a friend we can find."

"No, no." Said Sir Pelican, "Most grave, most dire.
To be without Friend or Fire in the heart.
Even on your birthday, how sad, how forlorn.
But No, No, No!
I cannot be a FRIEND to a BIG UGLY DRAGON
You must think me mad, or a tad bit not smart."

So, yet again, our secret most friend, a beauty nonetheless,
But no one could be told. She was so, so sad.
And like the Star of her name, kept trying, kept trying,
Though no one was buying.

Then from a GUM TREE FOREST
Came a Little Freddy Mouse.
Happily, left his house, Freddy Mouse
Sat on an Old Tree Stump.

"Mr. Fred the Mouse, Sir…
Today is my BIRTHDAY, will you be my FRIEND?"

"Simply No, No, No!
Chirped the mouse, you have no cheese!
And no BEAUTY to be behold…
Or so I have been told…
Go away before I change my mind.
For no UGLIER DRAGON can we find."

Completely saddened like a wet old towel,
Lypptuss the GUM TREE Dragon
Rested for a moment, no energy to fly, trot, or run…

Then a GOOD THOUGHT came into mind…
"If no one is around, and no friend to find,
Then I will WISH up a good soul of my OWN KIND…

So Lypptuss found a most beautiful wishing well
Of water so pure, so clean, and refreshing.
"Let me speak these magic words," she said.
"Let me sing, let me dance!
To this Water Well, let these words be my spell.
A FRIEND I SEE, A FRIEND TO BE…"

She CLOSED her eyes oh so tight…
She PULLED in her long arms and tail…
She wished, and wished, and WISHED to take flight…
Until her EYEBALLS were near to fail…

Then peeking with just one eye open,
Lypptuss looked down into the Water.
Nothing much she could see… But a wiggle, a wobble.
She signed a deep sadness, "Even my wishes don't reap.
Not even myself wants to be FRIEND to me!"

Still sad, still feeling down, Lypptuss the Dragon
Perched beside a BILLABONG
And she cried many tears, howled and sighed…
Sobbing, and crying, and so lonely inside.

"Well…" She said, "I best be going home now."
She thought in her mind, "No FRIEND, not even ONE."
Then looking up, "Only the GUM TREES sing today.
This will make me seek to stop this sorry weep…"

Holding up her head, she turned once, then again,
And once more! She turned, and turned, and churned
Out a BIG CIRCLE.

LYPPTUSS flapped her wings and wagged her tail.
"This is my PRIVATE BIRTHDAY.
No matter the trail of so many 'no, no, no's'
Oh, and what terrible travail…"

Then alone but holding her head high, she said,
"I guess I am TOO BIG, TOO UGLY, for sure."

Just then, as she WALKED with heavy steps, slow and sad,
Lypptuss TURNED a corner toward home.
Strange sounds she could hear, from afar, or were they near?
Right there, right then,
Lypptuss stopped short.

"Oh, my goodness.
What be that???
Can this be???
At all be true???
Or is the Wishing Well
Giving me a trick, or three, or two?"

For there before her BIG UGLY EYES
Were ALL and EVERY and MOST and MORE
GATHERED around a ONE HUGE CAKE
And that be REAL. That's for SURE.

Frog,
Tadpoles,
Mouse,
Pelican,
Koala,
And the Old Gum Tree.
Believe me or not.
Up to you.
But it be true.

Lypptuss the GUM TREE DRAGON
Licked her chops,
Smiled the BIGGEST SMILE and CLEVER.
"My FRIENDS," she said.
"This is the BEST BIRTHDAY EVER."

Then they all SANG together,
"Happy Birthday to you. Happy Birthday to you.
Happy Birthday Dear Lypptuss. Happy Birthday to you!"

The moral of this story, let me guess?
Let me say?
Is no matter how big, small, ugly, or fair;
You have a BEAUTY at play.

You are a beasty, a DRAGON, come what may.
And no one in this world can turn you away
From the wealth, magic, and power inside.
From your self's most self you cannot hide.

Remember the water hole, the well, the lake.
Remember to drink of water, as many tears you make.

CELEBRATE your SMILE and your HEART.

One day we will all be FRIENDS, mates, and not to part.
Yes, this is true blue. Our future. Our fate.

This is Lypptuss Dragon Dreaming.

www.ingramcontent.com/pod-product-compliance
Lightning Source LLC
Chambersburg PA
CBHW041922160426

42812CB00102B/2526